King James Version

El Mouatamid Ben Rochd

2024

"I will raise them up a Prophet from among their brethren, like unto thee, and I will put my words in his mouth; and he shall speak unto them all that I shall command him. And it shall come to pass, that whosoever will not hearken unto my words which he shall speak in my name, *I will require it of him.*"

[Deuteronomy 18:18]

CONTENTS
INTRODUCTION 5
PRINCIPLES 9
    Love
    Peace
    Original Sin
    Crucifixion
    Transubstantiation
    Trinity
    Celibacy
    Missionary Work
HISTORY 21
    Romans
    Essences
    Jesus
    Paul
    Constantine the Great
    Urban II
    Isabella & Ferdinand
    Martin Luther
    Henry VIII
    Caner & Caner
    Pope Benedict XVI
BOOKS 37
    Septuagint
    Catholic Bible
    King James Version
    Jehovah's witnesses'
    Book of Mormons
    Dead Sea Scrolls
    Saint Barnabas' Bible
    Symbolism
GROUPS 47
    North African Arianism
    Christian Arabs
    Catholics
    Orthodox
    Gnostics
AMERICAN FUNDAMENTALISM 55
    Christian Scientists
    Mormons
    Jehovah's Witnesses'
    Amish
    Other Sects
    Pentecostals

    Baptists
    Church of Scientology

CONCLUSION   67
Bible Succinct   93
History Succinct   103
Glossary   105
Bibliography   115

INTRODUCTION

'Why be interested in the study of Christianism', you may ask? Its study is crucial as it is, chronologically, the second major heritage of European thought; second in time after the Greco-Romans but most probably first in importance. Some of its principles are: Original Sin, Trinity, Crucifixion, Grace, Love and Forgiveness. Jesus said, 'you have heard that it was said, 'an eye for an eye, and a tooth for a tooth. But I say unto you, That ye resist no evil: but so ever shall smite thee on thy right cheek, turn to him the other also' (Matthew 5:39). See also (John 3:16)

In its first three centuries, Christianism was most unwelcome in pagan Roman Empire. The two sides bumped into each other face-to-face (do not the Christians believe that Jesus Christ was crucified by the Romans? And so was Paul indeed). From the purely intellectual aspect, many Greek notions infiltrated the Christian creed such as trinity, the eternity of the soul and the fate of man after death, to the point in which sincere Christians used to wonder 'what could combine light with darkness; to put the religion of Jesus together with the philosophy of the pagan Greeks?'

After a while, Christianity took root in Rome and became known as the Roman Catholic Church, thanks to Constantine the Great in 325. It had all the power and money of mighty Rome at hand. Its hierarchy became so materialistic and corrupt to the extent that the church owned large lands that were as big as half France and Germany put together. Religious interactions were based on gifts and bribery. Some Popes recognized their sons in spite of declared celibacy like Alexander VI [Rodrigo Borgia, d.1503]. Some Popes lived for war and arts merely like Julius II [Guiliano della Rovere, d. 1513]. German clergymen, in particular, used to take many concubines in spite of their supposed celibacy. Money became the center of the church life to the extent that it was said, 'no priest will ring a bell without money!'

Today we witness a mushrooming of religious fundamentalism all over the world, which is often narcissist and violent. As a matter of fact, 'Fundamentalism' is a purely American term. It was initiated at Niagara Bible Conference by James Inglis, a New York Baptist minister. During this big Protestant gathering, it was decided to write a few books setting *the foundations* of the world's 're-Christening'. That was the starting point of fundamentalism; i.e. the movement of Evangelists who believe that the Bible is 100% accurate and that it should be implemented in life and preached to all nations. They also call themselves the 'Moral Majority' in America. Some of their big leaders are Billy Graham, Fallwell, but the richest, most outstanding and media star is/was(?) American Jimmy Swaggart before he had a dramatic morality affair.

    To understand religion in America, one has to go back to England in the 16th c. Originally English King Henry 8th (1491-1547) had some tribulations with the Pope in Rome. The latter had exclusive and absolute divine right of interpretation over the Bible. The English king tried to marry Catherine of Aragon, his bother's widow; so as to unite Spain and England. This marriage was at first refused by the Pope. Then a dispensation was granted; since to marry a widow or divorced woman is badly seen in Christianity (Matthew 19:9). To make things worse Henry the 8th wanted to divorce her as she did not bear him the son he needed so badly; as heir of the British crown. Because of his problems with the Pope, he was self-appointed founder and head of the Church of England. He remarried, took 6 wives, then beheaded Anne Boleyn (for adultery) along with other wives. Within the English society -

turned protestant- some were dissatisfied. Those were the Puritans who sought more reform, simplicity of creed and worship. They were seeking freedom of belief. Because of persecution, they left England to Leiden, then took the Mayflower in 1620 to New England and ended in what came to be known as Providence State. The vital point about the Pilgrims is that their search for freedom of belief is what dubbed them 'Founding Fathers' and made them the pride of Americans. Their settlement in America is controversial as far as their relationship with the Native Americans is concerned.

The fact that America is the land of freedom and the fact that the Protestants deny the Pope any divine authority as far as the interpretation of the Bible is concerned, led to an incredible and 'savage' mushrooming of Christian sects; the most famous of which are the Christian Scientists, the Mormons, the Amish and the Jehovah's Witnesses. Lately Anglican David Jenkins recognized the manhood of Jesus (* see Appendix)

[MOST QUOTATIONS ARE FROM KJV]

PRINCIPLES

Some of the outstanding principles of Christianity are love, peace, salvation through the blood of Jesus, original sin, trinity, etc.

Love
Some Christians like to define their religion as the 'love of God and the love of man.' When Jesus was asked to sum up his religion, he answered, 'love Thy Lord and thy neighbor.' All the rest is just means to achieve this love. This is the reason why John 3:16 is the most crucial verse in the Bible, 'For God so loved the world, that he gave his only begotten son, that whosoever beliveth in him should not perish, but have everlasting life.'

The mutual love between God and the Christians is established. Love, charity and the clearing of hearts before any endeavor is necessary. Before they proceed to the communion, i.e. 'breaking bread and drinking wine,' Christians start by mutual criticism and complete reconciliation.

Jesus ordered them to love even their enemies from among the Jews and the Romans (including Saul who would later on

turn to Saint Paul). Jesus said, 'Ye have heard that it hath been said, Thou shalt love thy neighbor, and hate thine enemy.
However, I say to you: continue to love your enemies and to pray for those persecuting you. That you may prove yourselves sons of Your Father who is in the heavens.' Matthew 5:44

'Sonhood' has to be understood metaphorically.

Peace
Peace is another important feature of Christianity. Ever since his birth, Jesus was bestowed with peace, 'And this shall be a sign unto you; Ye shall find the babe wrapped in swaddling clothes, lying in a manger. And suddenly there was with the angel a multitude of the heavenly host praising God, and saying, Glory to God in the highest, and on earth peace, good will toward men.' Luke 2:14

Jesus himself praised the peacemakers, 'Blessed are the peacemakers: for they shall be called the children of God.' Matthew 5:9. He ordered one of his disciples, who took the sword, 'Put up again thy sword into his place: for all they that take the sword shall perish with the sword.' Matthew 26:52 He also ordered them, 'Whoever slaps you on the right cheek turn the other to him.' Matthew 5:39

Therefore, peace is the outstanding feature in Christianism, 'But the Comforter, which is the Holy Ghost, whom the Father will send in my name, he shall teach you all things, and bring all things to your remembrance, whatsoever I have said unto you. Peace I leave with you, my peace I give unto you' John 14:26

Original Sin

One of the most important principles in Christianity if not the most important is Original Sin. Adam disobeyed God and the whole humankind must go to hell!

You read in the Old Testament, 'Now the serpent was subtil than any beast of the field which the Lord God had made. And he said unto the woman, Yea, hath God said, Ye shall not eat of every tree of the garden? And the woman said unto the serpent, We may eat of the fruit of the trees of the garden: But of the fruit of the tree which is in the midst of the garden, God hath said, Ye shall not eat of it, neither shall ye touch it, lest ye die. And the serpent said unto the woman, Ye shall not surely die: For God doth know that in the day ye eat thereof, then your eyes shall be opened, and ye shall be as gods, knowing good and evil. And when the woman saw that the tree was good for food, and that it was pleasant to the eyes, and a tree to be desired to make one wise, she took of the fruit thereof, and did eat, and gave also unto her husband with her; and he did eat. And the eyes of them both were opened, and they knew that thy were naked; and they sewed fig leaves together, and made themselves aprons. And they heard the voice of the Lord God walking in the garden in the cool of the day: and Adam and his wife hid themselves from the presence of the Lord God amongst the trees of the garden. And the Lord God called unto Adam, and said unto him, Where art thou? And he said, I heard thy voice in the garden, and I was afraid, because I was naked; and I hid myself. And he said, Who told thee that thou was naked? Hast thou eaten of the tree, whereof I commanded thee that thou shouldest not eat? And the man, The woman whom thou gavest to be with me, she gave me of the tree, and I did eat. And the Lord God said unto the woman, What is this that thou hast done? And the woman said, The serpent beguilded me, and I did eat. And the Lord God said unto the serpent, Because thou hast done this, thou art cursed above all cattle, and above all beast of the field; upon thy belly shalt thou go, and dust shalt thou eat all the days of thy life: and I will put enmity between thee and the woman, and between thy seed and her seed; it shall bruise thy head, and thou shalt bruise his heel. Unto the woman he said, I will greatly multiply thy sorrow and thy conception, in sorrow thou shalt bring forth children; and thy desire shall be to thy husband, and he shall rule over thee. And unto Adam he said, Because thou hast hearken unto the voice of thy wife, and hast eaten of the tree, of which I commanded thee, saying, Thou shalt not eat of it: cursed is the ground for thy sake; in sorrow shalt thou eat of it all days of thy life; thorns also and thistles shall it bring forth to thee; and thou shalt eat the herb of the field; in the sweat of thy face shalt thou eat bread, till thou return unto the ground' Genesis 3

The only way out of the curse of Original Sin, according to the Christians is to believe in Christ's Crucifixion. According to Caner & Caner (2002, p. 150) original sin deserved *extreme penalty* either Christ blood on the cross or humanity domed to hell in its totality. There is no other way!

Crucifixion
Belief in Crucifixion is a must in Christianity. The Bible narrates how Jesus

was taken by the Jews to the Romans to be crucified. He died on the cross crying (blood?) for rescue from his Heavenly Father, 'Eloi, Eloi, lama sabachthani? which is, being interpreted, My God, my God, why hast thou forsaken me?' Marc 15:34

The Christians believe that is was that blood of Jesus that has saved them from Adam's original sin. It is known as Salvation through the Blood of Jesus. The only way to salvation is through that blood. An adulterous woman came to Jesus, he said to her, She said, No man, Lord. And Jesus said unto her, Neither do I condemn thee: go and sin no more.' John 8:11. Jesus required his disciples to look for the sinners, 'for I am not come to call the righteous, but sinners to repentance.' Mathew 9:13.

Salvation is also obtained through Baptism, 'He that believeth and is baptized shall be saved.' Marc 16:16

Transubstantiation
Christians believe that bread and wine, when consumed are transformed into the body and blood of Jesus. Some Moroccan evangelists gather for transubstantiation after 'clearing their hearts of all individual grudges, before they start communion with

Jesus through bread and wine(?)'. (According to Tihad Shtiraki 23 June 2001)

This takes place in emulation of Jesus' Last Supper. His blood is believed to be the price paid for original sin on the cross.

During Jesus' Last Supper, he taught his disciples a few final points about him, his betrayal and the Coming Comforter. 'Why trouble ye the woman? For she hath wrought a good work upon me…now the first day of the feast of unleavened bread the disciples came to Jesus, saying unto him, Where wilt thou that we prepare for thee to eat the Passover? And he said, Go into the city to such a man, and say unto him, The Master saith, My time is at hand; I will keep the Passover at thy house with my disciples. And the disciples did as Jesus had appointed them; and they made ready the Passover. Now when the even was come, he sat down with the twelve. And as they did eat, he said, Verily I say unto you, that one of you shall betray me. And they were exceeding sorrowful, and began every one of them to say unto him, Lord, is it i? and he answered and said, He that dippeth his hand with me in the dish, the same shall betray me. The Son of man goeth as it is written of him: but woe unto that man by whom the Son of man is betrayed! It had been good for that man if he had not been born. Then Judas, which betrayed him, answered and said, Master, is it I? he said unto him, Thou hast said. And as they were eating, Jesus took bread, and blessed it, and brake it, and gave it to the disciples, and said, Take, eat, this is my body. And he took the cup, and gave thanks and gave it to them, saying, Drink ye all of it; For this is my blood of the new testament, which is shed for many for the remission of sins. But I say unto you, I will not drink henceforth of this fruit of the vine, until that day when I drink it new with you in my Father's kingdom. And when they had sung an hymn, they went out into the mount of Olives. Matthew 26:6

Trinity

Christians believe in Trinity i.e. three gods united in one. It was first 'the Father and the Son,' then 'the Holy Ghost' was added. Many rows and troubles were caused by this belief amongst Christian groups themselves.

'The article of faith up until about 250 A.D. was, "I believe in God, the Almighty." Between 180 and 210 A.D. the word "Father" was added before the "Almighty." This was bitterly contested by a number of the leaders of the Church. Bishop Victor and Bishop

Zephysius are on record as condemning this movement.' Ata ur-rahim (1979, p.9)

At first the Roman emperors such as Nero and Diocletian used to persecute Christians in the most cruel fashions imaginable, such as Nero's human candles. But after Nicea (325) the opposite prevailed; Roman law condemned and executed anyone who would not believe in Christian trinity.

The verse says, 'Go therefore and make disciples of all nations, baptizing them in the name of the Father and the Son and the Holy Ghost (Matthew 28:19)

But the Jehovah's Witnesses reject trinity as from Roman paganism (or even Egyptian paganism!). Their arguments are as follows:
1. the Gospel says, 'And this is life eternal, that they might know thee only true God, and Jesus Christ, whom thou hast sent' John 17:3
2. some consider it from pagan origin i.e. the three Roman gods Jove, Juno and Minerva.
3. God is no confusion deity 'for God is not *the author* of confusion, but of peace, as in all churches of the saints.' 1Corinthinas 14:33

4. no trace of trinity in the Old Testament
5. no trace of trinity in the New Testament either
6. neither Jesus nor Paul taught it
7. Martyr Justin (165) considered Jesus an angel rather than a god
8. Constantine the Great decided that 'the Son and the Father were of the same spirit, not trinity. Although he himself ignored all of theology. Later 'the Holy Spirit' was added.

Celibacy

Celibacy (Monasticism) is one principle of the Catholic Church in particular. It is based on the fact that Jesus never married and on Paul's teachings, 'I say therefore to the unmarried and widows, it is good for them if they abide even as I.' I Corinthians 7:8

It has faced many bitter problems as in recruiting priests. American Catholic Church found it self forced to import Irish priests. Celibacy goes in fact against the teachings of the Bible itself, which encourage polygamy itself.

Missionary Work

The Christians insist that there is no prophet after Christ by quoting the verse, 'Thomas saith unto him, Lord, we know not with thou goest; and how can we know the way? Jesus saith unto him, I am the way, the truth, and the life: no man cometh unto the Father, but by me.' John 14:6 And his saying, 'I am alpha and omega, the first and the last.' Revelation 1:8

Christians encourage worldwide missionary work by quoting 'Go ye therefore, and teach all nations, baptizing them in the name of the Father, and of the Son, and of the Holy Ghost.' Matthew 28:19

HISTORY

Romans

As far as Greco-Roman culture is concerned, historians have agreed that, the Romans defeated the their Greek neighbors militarily and overpowered them. But the Greeks invaded the Roman mind by their philosophy, mythology and poetry. The victor and the defeated became eventually one culture known as Greco-Romans. Christianity was born in the midst of the Roman Empire.

Christianity was born in the Roman Empire. The Romans used to control the whole Mediterranean sea, including North Africa, which was considered as the 'grain store of Rome.' it was the place where they used to take their grains and slaves.

Essenes

The Romans ruled the south coast as well as the north coast of the Mediterranean Sea considering north Africa as their grain and slave store. They had their own religion which worshipped Jupiter and were striving to force it on their colonies by force. They succeeded to a large extent except with the "The chosen People" i.e. the Jews.

The Jews have been battered all along their history by a series of invaders of Palestine. Because of their successive and continual defeats the hatred towards humanity filled their hearts. Some of the Bible passages are all but complaints and cries to Jehovah. Other sections are bitter wishes for revenge and the downfall of their enemies. But some Jews retained their mind balance even in the darkest days of their big ordeal. These continued in the hope of receiving the new Moses. (Deuteronomy 18:18). He would be their anointed king and savior!

In their struggle against Roman assimilation, the Jews divided into three trends; Pharisees, Sadducees and Essenes i.e. those who accepted complete assimilation; they became Romans, acquired wealth and made the best of a bad bargain, they acquired wealth and position both temporally and religiously. Others opted for a marriage of convenience with mighty Rome, they became half Romans half Jewish, i.e. hypocrites and also benefited in the temporal as well as the religious planes.

There was a third Jewish group though, who differed from the first two categorically. They took to the mountains to free themselves from the Roman pagan law [Malcolm X] and tyrannical rule. They also achieved more importantly the direct contact with Jehovah! They lived by the Torah and prepared themselves for the fight with the invaders of the holy land. They were wanted by the Romans, who failed to find their hideouts.

Those Jewish patriots grew in number although they respected strict celibacy.

Jesus
Jesus was born in Bethlehem rather than in Nazareth in Judea in the time of Roman king Herod, who had decided to kill all Jewish babies. His adoptive father Joseph went up to Nazareth, which is called Bethlehem to get registered with Mary. Jesus was born in a manger as Mary and Joseph did not find anywhere to stay for the night. And suddenly there was with the angel a multitude of the heavenly host praising God.

Jesus lived as a simple Jewish rabbi worshipping God in Jerusalem. When he was 30 years of age his mission started. He met his cousin John the Baptist who baptized him in the Jordan River and the Holy Ghost descended on him as a dove. He toured Jericho, Judea spreading his message about 'the Kingdom of Heaven' and performed miracles curing the sick without pay (Mathew 8:20). He educated his 12 disciples by stories, parables and proverbs from everyday life. In his Mount Olive sermon he taught how top pray and how to praise the 'Sacred Name of God.' love, humility and repentance were the backbones of his teachings (John 13:33). Then he departed them promising that he will be back on the condition, 'if you love me rejoice I will go to my father because my father is greater than me' John 14:6 [Jehovah's Witnesses Version]

Paul (- ?67) *Original Sin*
Paul was the 1st Christian missionary to the gentiles. He died as a martyr in Rome. He advocated most (if not all) the above mentioned principles of Christianity.

According to Christian magazine The *Plain Truth*, the ideas Paul boldly taught the Greeks are still revolutionary today. About 50 AD, a spiritual crusade began in Greece that dramatically changed the tide of history. The apostle Paul landed on the European continent, armed with the gospel message given to him by Jesus Christ. This project was so important to God that he miraculously led Paul to Europe to teach the message of salvation, beginning in Macedonian Greece.

Luke, Paul's traveling companion, explained that Paul had been prevented from preaching in certain areas of Asia Minor, today Western Turkey: 'A vision appeared to Paul in the night,' Luke wrote. 'A man in Macedonia stood and pleaded with him, saying, "come over to Macedonia and help us" (Acts 16:6-9).

What did Paul teach that so revolutionized the religious and philosophical thinking of the European continent? Why should we, living almost 2,000 years later in a very different world, be interested in this message?

In a letter to the church in Greek city of Corinth, the apostle Paul wrote: 'I determined not to know anything among you except Jesus Christ and him crucified' (I Corinthians 2:2)

(*The Plain Truth*, Apr. 1992)

Other sources narrate a different version of the story. Paul made a dramatic conversion from Judaism to Christianism because of a vision he had on his way to Damascus. Not long before all these events took place, it is recorded that Paul had desired to marry a woman called Popea, who was the attractive but ambitious daughter of the high priest of the Jews. She possessed haunting beauty and an intriguing mind. She liked Paul, but she rejected his offers of marriage and went to Rome as an actress. Starting on the stage, she climbed step by step until she reached Nero's bed. Ultimately she married him and so became the empress of the Roman Empire. Paul therefore had good reason to resent both the Jews and the Romans. Paul's conversion coincided with his being rejected by Popea. He must have been under considerable emotional and mental strain at the time. It is possible that this crisis in his life had some bearing on this sudden change from his being one of the greatest supporters of the Jewish Law to one of its greatest enemies.

Paul had a special philosophy in spreading the truth of Christianism as he confessed, 'for if the truth of God hath more abounded through my lie unto His glory; why yet I am also judged a sinner? (Romans 3:7)

After Paul and disciple Saint Barnabas split, and so Christianity took at least two forms: Unitarian and Trinitarian Christianisms, besides numerous Gospels.

Constantine the Great (?280-337)
'Turn the Other Cheek?'

Constantine was the 1st Christian emperor of the Roman Empire. He had once a vision of a cross in the sky, and turned Pauline Christianity from a persecuted religion (cf. Diocletian) to a dominant (viz. persecuting to the Jews) Church. He established Sunday into a holiday (sun-God of the Romans) as opposed to the Jewish Sabbath on Saturday. He met (opposed) Arius, at the Council of Nicea 325. It was then that the (Pauline) Nicean creed was adopted. His decrees established the major beliefs and certain social occupations such as serfs that were permanently attached to the land. Constantine was cruel even to his own family members (he killed both his son and wife). Historically, he is more important than Alexander, Napoleon or Hitler, because of the enduring influence of his policies! (*The 100*, p. 107)

The life of Libyan Unitarian priest Arius is so much intertwined with the life of Emperor Constantine that it is not possible to understand one without knowing the other. The story of how Constantine first became involved with the Christian church began in Rome.

Constantine became jealous of his elder son and heir, Crispus. The young prince had become very popular because of his good looks, his charming manner and his bravery on the field of battle. To make sure of his position as emperor, Constantine had him murdered. The death of Crispus cast a gloom over the whole realm. It was known that the step mother of Crispus had wanted her own son to succeed Constantine. She therefore had motive for killing Crispus. Constantine accordingly put the blame for his crime on her, and killed her by immersing her in a bath full of hot water. He hoped to mitigate one crime by the other. The result however, was just the opposite of what he had planned – the supporters of the dead queen joined forces with the followers of the dead son, and both sought revenge. In desperation he turned to the priests of the Roman Temple of Jupiter for help, but they told him that there was no sacrifice or prayer which could absolve him from the two murders. It became so uncomfortable to be in Rome that Constantine decided to go to Byzantium.

On his arrival there, he renamed the city after himself, and called it Constantinople. He met with unexpected success from the Pauline church; its leaders told him that if he did penance in their Church, his sins would be forgiven. Constantine made full use of this facility. His hands were not only stained with the blood from two murders, but were also full of the problems of governing his empire.

The mighty Roman Catholic Church was born and well-established for centuries until the protest of Reformation leaders, such as Martin Luther, arrived on scene.

Urban II (1042-1099) *the Crusades*

Khalif Omar conquered Jerusalem without bloodshed in a most magnanimous fashion (cf. Gibb) leaving the Holy City to its own people. As far the re-conquest to the 'Tomb of Jesus' the mighty horrific Crusades were declared by French Pope Urban II from Clermont.

According to Zainab Abd Aziz the crusades were a mixture of military, political, religious and economic tactics and struggles that were unique in human history. The Pope himself was fighting the emperor for the power over the European peoples, its kings and spiritual leaders. He aimed at uniting the Christian world though a common goal and method. One of the main goals of the crusades was to render the Arab world into a

European world vassal which would be catholic in religion and Latin in language.

There has been some 8 crusades at least. The first one was declared by French Pope Urban II (1042-1099) starting from his fiery talk in Clermont in France. He urged monk Peter the Venerable to enter Jerusalem for the re-conquest the 'tomb of Jesus!' the Jews suffered this catholic campaign as well as the orthodox Christians. When the crusading armies reached Jerusalem 70, 000 Muslims were slaughtered (Judd, History of Civilization, 1966)

Isabella & Ferdinand (1942) *The Inquisition*

Within Europe itself the mighty Catholic Church was in total iron control unlike most religions. It had a well structured hierarchy. She had destroyed all rival Christian groups in most bloodiest way imaginable. This was known as the darkest page in European history. It was the *Inquisition*!

Inquisition reached its climax in 12th c. when Pope Gregory IX decreed a life sentence to anyone who 'confessed his sin and death on anyone who did not.' The confession were obtained by pulling out people's nails as a means!

Inquisition was especially linked to the name of Spanish queen Isabella (1451-1504) who married King Ferdinand. She established Spanish universities. Those were like Islamic universities as far as form was concerned. She also developed the ecclesiastic class and *nicely* innovated Spanish Inquisition! This was a chilling law against freedom of speech and even thought, the outcome of which was tragic expelled of the Jews and Muslims from Grenada (1492) [cf. The Story of the Key]. She also urged Christopher Columbus to discover America in the same year.

Martin Luther *Reformation* (1483-1546)

Martin Luther was born in Germany. He received a good university education and studied law. He decided to become a monk, got a PhD in theology from the University of Wittenberg and soon joined its faculty. After a trip to Rome, his grudge against Catholicism grew when he saw the worldly vanity of its clergy. He resented their wealth and privileges and above all resented their practice of indulgences as penalty for sin. On October 31, 1517, he nailed a list of 95 theses on the door of Wittenberg Church before disappearing from mighty Roman Catholic Church reprisals.

He married Sister Katharina Von Bora and urged the lords to crash the rebellion of the peasants. Some of his notorious books are *Babylonian Captivity* 1520, *Christian Liberty* 1520. His major contribution is his translation of the Bible from Latin into the German language.

His doctrine is that the Bible is the only authority in answering religious questions. Salvation, according to him, can be obtained through the trust in the limitless grace and goodness of God only. Belief in God is all that matters.

The Lutherans are 100 million in the world especially in Germany, the USA and the Scandinavian countries (where the Lutheran Church stands for state religion).

King Henry VIII

In the 16th century, English King Henry VIII wanted to divorce his Spanish wife Catherine of Aragon and remarry, but as a catholic he had to turn to the Roman Catholic Church for permission. Rome was reluctant because it considers marriage to be a divine bond that can only be undone by God in the hereafter. He divorced her, remarried, executed his second wife and then declared himself the Head of Church of England. (cf. Rev. David Jenkins)

The split was at first done for personal reasons but later developed to give the Protestant trend that reviewed the Catholic Bible by expunging 7 of its books considered as apocrypha, and revised some of the Catholic dogmas.

This split with the Roman Catholic Church was known as the Reformation. In Germany, Calvin and Martin Luther led it. This led to the Protestant Churches rather than Church, since each person was entitled to read the Bible and understand it his own way, by contrast with the exclusivism of the Pope in Rome who was supposed to be the unique infallible interpreter of the Bible.

The Protestant Churches did not really protest against the dogmas of the Catholic Church as they kept the most important of which, like 'original sin', 'trinity', 'crucifixion', etc.. They came to challenge the power of Rome only to develop their own. So in England for instance where the Anglican Church became State Church, the missionary work was usually mixed with British

Intelligence. The priests sent to India – ruled by Islam for centuries (712-1743)– were there to pave the way for the military invasion.

Caner & Caner (2002)

After the 11 September attacks [see Thierry Meyssan, l'Effroyable imposture] two professors from the university of Texas and the university of north Carolina named Caner & Caner published their book entitled Unveiling Islam. Their goal is twofold: to present different aspects of Islam and to preach the 'true religion' to the one billion Muslims through out the world. The authors opted for a hard line criticism that reaches offensive limits and extreme blasphemy on several occasions. They criticized Jihad, the Prophet Muhammad, the Quran, Allah and the Muslim woman.

They use Aristotelian logic, especially the notion 'Excluded Middle' to prove that Christianism is superior to Islam. 'Islam and Christianity alike claim to hold the inerrant, infallible Word of God. yet according to Aristotle's law of non-contradiction () and law of the excluded middle () only three conclusions can be reached after viewing the evidence:

1. The Qur'an is the Word of God.
2. The Bible is the Word of God.
3. Neither is the Word of God.

The Qur'an and the Bible cannot both be the World of God, because God does not teach different and contradictory things at different points in history.' (C&C,p.229)

Pope Benedict XVI

The last show of hostility towards Islam came lately from German Pope Benedict XVI when he bitterly criticized prophet Muhammad , 'show me just what Mohammed brought that was new, and there you will find only evil and inhuman, such as his command to spread by the sword the faith he preached.'

Pope benedict XVI (a nickname) exposed the progress of Protestantism at the expense of Catholicism because of the reformation led by martin Luther. The latter movement spread all over Europe and north America and was embraced by most famous German intellectuals such as Goethe, Kant et al. he also insisted on rejecting Turkey from the European union as it has nothing to do with Europe which is according to him, a cultural union nor a geographical one.'

BOOKS

The Bible consists of two sections, viz. the Old Testament (the Torah) and the New Testament (the Evangels). This is the oldest book in the world and the bestseller. Its original languages were Hebrew and Greek. It was translated into hundreds if not thousands of languages, including Latin (JeRome 4 AD), English King James Version (19611) and Arabic in its many dialects. The Old Testament consists of the Books of Moses (Pentateuch), while the New Testament consists essentially of the four canonical books plus St. Paul's epistles.

Septuagint

The Septuagint t was probably the first translation in Greek. It dates from the third century B.C. and was written by Jews in Alexandria. It was on this text that the New Testament was based. It remains authoritative until the seventh century ad. The basic Greek texts in general use in the Christian world are from the manuscripts catalogued under the title Codex Vatinacus in the Vatican City and Codex Sinaiticus at the British museum, London. They date from the fourth century A.D.' (Bucaille p. 26)

Catholic Bible

The catholic Bible contains 7 more books than the KJV (protestant Bible) which are Tobit, Judith, I Maccabees, II Maccabees, Wisdom, Ben Sira and Baruch. It was translated in 420 by JeRome, a monk and a scholar. The translation was from the Hebrew and Greek Scriptures into Latin to give the vulgate or Catholic Bible.

King James Version (1611)

The notorious King James Version is described as 'easy-to-read, self-pronouncing, favorite for almost four centuries (...) It brings the extraordinary power and poetry of Scripture into life.' [cf. Ben Rochd (2000)]

The other side of the coin is to be found in, 'I argued for the theory that King James himself was the real poet who used the nom de plume Shakespeare. King James was brilliant. He was the greatest king who ever sat on the British throne...it was he who poetically 'fixed' the Bible – which in its present king James version has enslaved the world' (Malcolm X 1980)

Jehovah's Witnesses' *New World Translation*

The Jehovah's Bible starts as follows, 'it is a very responsible thing to translate the Holy Scriptures from their original languages of Hebrew, Aramaic and Greek into modern speech. Translating the Holy Scriptures means rendering into another language the thoughts and sayings of Jehovah God, the heavenly Author of this sacred library of sixty-six books that holy men long ago were inspired to write down for our benefit today..'

Still Jehovah's Witnesses' Bible is the worst against the Arabs. Isaiah 21:13 is rendered as, 'The pronouncement against the desert plain'. Compare with the same verse in the Catholic Bible, 'Against the Arabs,' the King James Version, 'the Burden upon Arabia', New American Standard Bible, 'The Oracle about Arabia', the Hebrew Bible, 'A Prophecy concerning Arabia', etc. amazing!

[I had a 30 second rift with them in Providence (Ri) about the /j/ sound in Hebrew. They said: "we'll talk to you later"]

Book of Mormons

The Book of Mormons is an enormous Bible (probably the biggest as it includes the Old Testament, the New Testament plus the Book of Mormons. It introduces itself as, 'it is an abridgment of the record of the people of Nephi, and also of the Lamanites –Written to the Lamanites, who are a remnant of the house of Israel; and also to Jew and gentile –Written by way of commandment, and Oslo by the sprit of prophecy and revelation – Written and sealed up, and hid up unto the Lord, that they might not be destroyed –to come forth by the gift and power of God unto the interpretation thereof –Sealed by the hand of Maroni...'

Dead Sea Scrolls

'In 1974, an Arab boy, tending his flock near Qumran, found one of the sheep was missing, so he decided to climb the nearby mountain in search of the missing animal. During his search, he came upon the mouth of a cave into which he thought the sheep had gone. He threw a stone into it and expected to hear stone hitting stone. Instead the stone made a clinking noise as if it had hit an earthen pot. His imagination was fired. H thought that perhaps he had stumbled upon a treasure trove. Next morning, he returned to the cave and, with a friend to help him, entered it. Instead they found several jars amongst the fragments of broken pottery. They took one of them to the camp where they were living and were bitterly disappointed when all that they found was a foul smelling leather scroll. They unrolled it until it reached from one side of the tent to the other. It was one of the scrolls which were later sold for a quarter of a million dollars. They sold it to a Syrian Christian named Kando for a few shillings. Kando was a cobbler, and he was only interested in the leather as it might come in handy for resolving old shoes. Kando, however, noticed that the leather sheet was over-written in letters unknown to him. after a closer look, he decided to show it to the Syrian metropolitan of saint mark's monastery in Jerusalem. These two shadowy figures carted the scrolls from one country to another, hoping to make money' (Ata, p. 22)

Saint Barnabas' Bible (Joseph)

Joseph (Saint Barnabas) was one of Jesus Christ's disciples if not their best, 'Then peter, turning about, seeth the disciple whom Jesus loved following; which also leaned on his breast at supper...this is the disciple which testifieth of these things, and wrote these things: and we know that this testimony is true.' John 21:20ff. 'And Joses, who by the apostles was surnamed Barnabas, (which is, being interpreted, The son of consolation,) a Levite, and of the country of Cyprus, Having land, sold it, and brought the money, and laid it at the apostles' feet.' Acts 4:36.

Saint Barnabas violently disagreed with st. Paul, 'And the contention was so sharp between them, that they departed asunder one from the other' Acts 15:39. he was never mentioned in the Bible after that event.

The gospel of Saint Barnabas is the only Gospel written by a direct disciple of Jesus Christ. The man spent most of his life with Jesus company during the three years of his ministry. Unfortunately it is not recognized as canonical by any church nowadays!

"The manuscript, from which the English translation of the Gospel of Barnabas was made, was originally in the possession of Pope Sextus (1589-1590). He had a friend, a monk called Fra Marino, who became very interested in the Gospel of Barnabas after reading the writings of Iraneus, who quoted from it extensively. One day he went to see the Pope, they lunched together and, after the meal, the Pope fell asleep. Father Merino began to browse through the books in the Pope's private library and discovered the Gospel of Barnabas. Concealing it in the sleeves of his robe, he left and came out of the Vatican with it. This manuscript then passed through hands until it reached "a person of great name and authority" in Amsterdam..." (Ata ur-Rahim 1979, p. 41)

Symbolism

K.J.V. and the Bible in general presents a beautiful piece of literature with its symbolism, metaphor, among other figures of speech. Such as the story of the ten virgins, symbols such as the camel entering the needle expressing the impossibility for the rich to enter paradise, Matthew 19:24, the useless mending an old clot with a new one meaning the vain defense of truth using falsehood Matthew 9:16, the symbol of fruit and new song, 'Sing unto the Lord a new song, and his praise from the end of the earth, ye that go down to the sea, and all that is therein; the isles, and the inhabitants thereof' Isaiah 42:10, the washing of hands, used by Pilate to clear himself of all responsibility of Jesus' blood, Matthew 27:24.

We will pick up a few of those symbols such as *serpent, mile, the way, the lamp, wine and bread, father, Son of Man, fruit tree, kingdom, gods*, etc. as in:

The snake represented Satan who led Eve and Adam astray, 'Now the serpent was subtil than any beast of the field which the Lord God had made. And he said unto the woman, Yea, hath God said, Ye shall not eat of every tree of the garden? And the woman said unto the serpent, We may eat of the fruit of the trees of the garden: But of the fruit of the tree which is in the midst of the garden, God hath said, Ye shall not eat of it, neither shall ye touch it, lest ye die. And the serpent said unto the woman, Ye shall not surely die: For God doth know that in the day ye eat thereof, then your eyes shall be opened, and ye shall be as gods, knowing good and evil.

It also represents Jesus' enemies, i.e. the spies, 'But when he saw many of the Pharisees and Sadducees come to his baptism, he said unto them, O generation of vipers, who hath warned you to flee from the wrath to come?' Matthew 37
'It is written, Man shall not live by bread alone, but by every word that proceedeth out of the mouth of God.' Matthew 4:4

The symbol of son of man that Jesus kept repeating over and over again, rather than son of God; as if he predicted how his followers would wrongly describe him after his departure. He as so humble in describing himself, 'The foxes have holes, and the birds of the air *have* nests, but the Son of man hath not where to lay *his* head.' Matthew 8:20

The symbol of the tree concerns the ministry of the Jews. 'in Matthew 21:19-21, Jesus spoke of the fruitless fig tree (A Biblical symbol of prophetic heritage) to be cleared after being given a last chance of three years (the duration of Jesus' ministry) to give fruit. In a later verse in the same chapter, Jesus said: I tell you that God's kingdom will be taken from you and given to people who will do what He commands' Matthew 21:43(Dr. Jamal Badawi))

Another symbol concerns them in their arrogance that of 'gods', 'If he called them gods ' John 10:35

GROUPS

Christianity never was one homogeneous group but rather many 'warring sects' to put is Guillaume's words (p. 14) and others. The main split in this religion was between Unitarian Christians and Trinitarian Christians. The most famous early Unitarian Christians were the followers of Arius, where the most famous of the Trinitarians were the Jacobites , who believed that Jesus had one nature which is deity with human characteristics.

Up until 180 AD the Christian belief was, 'I believe in the One Mighty God', then things started to change. Some joined the Son with the Father as 'wine and water other joined them as oil and water'...

North African Arianism

The North African Christians rejected Trinity violently. There lived a Libyan Unitarian priest called Arius. He was very thin and tall, handsome if not for his face pallor and short sight. His dress and life were those of an ascetic, taciturn until he broke in fiery word when defending the unity of God and the humanity of Christ. He was assassinated by Rome.

The North African Christians rebelled first being led by Donatus in 313. JeRome himself ' the undisputed leader above all arguments and forces among the inhabitants of north Africa.' Rome tried to decree a law to punish donatus and his followers, but the people of north Africa respected him more than Jesus himself. Rome considered the north Africans as 'dangerous people who respect neither law nor tradition.' By contrast the donatus considered the Roman priests as 'emissaries of Satan.'

The Nestorians were the followers of Nestor, patriarch of Constantinople (428-431) he drew a clear distinction between the creator and Jesus and rejected the label 'mother of god'. He was a follower of Arius and was excommunicated by Rome.

Christian Arabs

Christianity found as refuge in Arabia from very early age even as Saint Paul fell off the wall in Damascus, the same applies to Saint Thomas who founded a church in Iraq. There were also Christians in southern Arabia who first welcomed the Muslims migrants. In Hijaz itself there were Judam and Udra tribes. At the ka'aba itself thee was picture of Jesus and Mary. Prophet Muhammad did not want to destroy them although he destroyed all other idols and images. The prophet himself wore a garment offered by some Christians in the desert.

different Christian groups were fighting theological if not bloody wars about tenets of creed. Some of whom were Greek orthodox, Monophesites, Nestorians which is still availing nowadays. The Jacobites were very actively converting the Arab tribes before Islam. They built churches, fasted and helped the people of the desert. The convents were open day and night generously providing for the needs of the people.

By opposition, Greek orthodox were ruthless in their attitude towards the Arab Christians to the extent that they lost their control over Syria as the Syrian rejected the 'tow natures of Jesus.' Besides the Greeks looked down upon the Arabs, humiliated and even persecuted and killed the Christian Arabs.

According to Guillaume, 'the Greeks paved the way for their downfall. Within a century or so Muslim Arabs were at the gates of Constantinople, and its ultimate fall to the Turks in 1453 was the logical outcome of the shameful treatment of the Arab Christians by their orthodox rues. Their policy was as foolish as it was wicked. Henceforth they stood for tyranny and injustice in the eyes of the Arabs, and through them Christianity was associated with perfidy' (p.19)

Catholics

The Catholic Church was born a the hands of Roman Emperor Constantine the great [see above]. Its capital is the Vatican and its head is the Pope.

Vatican the smallest state in the world its dwellers are 830 people led by the Pope. It was a gift from Constantine the great to Pope Sylvester the first in the fourth century as the capital of the Catholic Church.

The word Pope is derived from Latin padre i.e. father which an ecclesiastic title given ever since the 8th c. to the priest of Rome as the head of the catholic church. He is considered as Christ's scribe of the universal church and jesus' servant.

Pope benedict XVI (a nickname) exposed the progress of Protestantism at the expense of Catholicism because of the reformation led by martin Luther. The latter movement spread all over Europe and north America and was embraced by most famous German intellectuals such as Goethe, Kant et al. he also insisted on rejecting Turkey from the European union as it has nothing to do with Europe which is according to him, a cultural union nor a geographical one.'

Orthodox

Constantine the great moved from Rome to beautiful Constantinople in the year 325 the split in the Roman Empire began between eastern and eastern parts of his empire. The differences were linguistic as well as theological at first. Constantine leaned more towards the eastern part as he felt more at ease rather than in Rome that did not forgive his sins (the killing of his son and wife in boiling water!)

Trinity posed extremely difficult intellectual problems to the different and fighting (Guillaume, p.68) groups. At the council of Nicea 451, they discussed the nature of Christ, or rather his 'natures'. The western church accepted its doctrine Nicean doctrine, but the Eastern Church rejected it. So that was the internal spilt of the catholic church. The Egyptian Copts split as well as the Syrian Jacobites and the Armenians.

Another big intellectual problem ensued when the last person 'Holy Ghost' was added to the Father and the Son. The Holy Ghost was considered as born from both according to the Roman Church. The Church of Constantinople rebelled against this addition in 876. they rejected the universality and rule of the Pope and his laws. As a reaction Rome excommunicated the Eastern Patriarch and the latter cursed the Pope. From that spilt were born most Orthodox Churches such as the Russian, Polish, Serbian…, which were in turn independent of each other! The orthodox rebellion was also stamped by an Iconoclast rebellion as well as they believed that 'God can not be described or limited to a picture.'

Gnostics

Catholic Church weakened after having violently repressed all 'heretics' such as north African churches Arianism, Donatism, Gnostics, etc.

The Gnostics claimed to be able to know God directly without the mediation of the church!

They believed that 'the man who knows himself knows his Creator!' Their idea was simple: since we have been created at the image of God and of His spirit, his Truth is within us. We can reach Him though personal spiritual and physical experiences including the most trivial.

At this point in my musings, I came upon another reference to north Africa which was like a searchlight ion the subject. This was the phenomenon of the Christian Gnostics. Gnosis means 'knowledge' or 'insight'. The word is applied to those Christians who relied on their own spiritual resources, their personal insights, to discover their relationship with God. this automatically placed them at loggerheads with the authority of the established Church which, naturally, wished to maintain the monopoly of the 'truth' and the graces by which people could achieve it. Gnostics were at the extreme end of a spectrum of belief which tended to disagree with the idea that the 'Church' was the sole mediator between god and man. They further had very jaundice view of the world, considering it to be essentially evil and their aim was to separate the 'divine spark' from the material world. Among Gnostic sects were my old friends the Manichaens, the Canthars, the Mandeans and many others described as heretics. What intrigued me about some of these was a description of their rituals which suggested to me a direct connection with the Sheela na Gigs.' (Bob Quinn, p. 170)

This is why the Catholic Church felt threatened by these groups, as they undermined its very foundation. It used to stand between the believers and God by its ecclesiastic hierarchy and political authority. These 'Sufis' believed that 'your love to anything more than God is a blasphemy!'

AMERICAN FUNDAMENTALISM

'Fundamentalism' is a purely American term. It was initiated at Niagara Bible Conference by James Inglis, a New York Baptist minister. During this big protestant gathering, it was decided to write a few books setting *the foundations* of the world's 're-Christening'. That was the starting point of fundamentalism; i.e. the movement of Evangelists who believe that the Bible is 100% accurate and that it should be implemented in life and preached to all nations. They also call themselves the 'Moral Majority' in America. Some of their big leaders are Billy Graham, Fallwell, but the richest, most outstanding and media star is/was(?) American Jimmy Swaggart before he had a dramatic morality affair.

To understand religion in America, one has to go back to England in the 16th c. Originally English King Henry 8th (1491-1547) had some tribulations with the Pope in Rome. The latter has exclusive and absolute divine right of interpretation over the Bible. The English king tried to marry Catherine of Aragon, his bother's widow; so as to unite Spain and England. This marriage was at first refused by the Pope. Then a dispensation was granted; since to marry a widow or divorced woman is badly seen in Christianity (Matthew 19:9). To make things worse Henry the 8th wanted to divorce her as she bore him not the son needed so badly; as heir of the British crown. Because of his problems with the Pope, he was self-appointed founder and head of the Church of England. He remarried, took 6 wives, then beheaded Anne Boleyn (for adultery) along with other wives. Within the English society - turned protestant- some were dissatisfied. Those were the Puritans who sought more reform, simplicity of creed and worship. They were seeking freedom of belief. Because of persecution, they left England to Leiden, then took the Mayflower in 1620 to New England and ended in what came to be known as Providence State. The vital point about the Pilgrims is that their search for freedom of belief is what dubbed them 'Founding Fathers' and made them the pride of Americans. Their settlement in America is controversial as far as their relationship with the Native Americans is concerned.

The fact that America is the land of freedom and the fact that the protestants deny the Pope any divine authority as far as the interpretation of the Bible is concerned, led to an incredible and 'savage' mushrooming of Christian sects; the most famous of which are the Christian Scientists, the Mormons, the Amish and the Jehovah's Witnesses. Lately Anglican David Jenkins recognized the manhood of Jesus (* see Appendix)

Christian Scientists *Prayer Heals* (1821-1910)

Mary Baker was born in New Hampshire in 1821. Her third husband was Esa Eddy who was one of her own followers. Being of weak physical constitution (if not sick!), she strongly believed that her recovery was only due to the true understanding of the Holy Scriptures.

She spent her whole life studying the spiritual idea of 'healing through prayer!' this gave her an important number of followers enough to make a sect. In 1875, she published her first book *Science and Health with a Key to Scriptures*. In 1879, she officially founded her Church world-widely known as Christ Scientist Church, in Boston. Three years later, she founded Massachusetts Metaphysical College destined to teach her doctrine. Ten years later, thanks to her expansion, she renamed her organization First Church of Christ Scientist, which is directed by the rules she set in her book *Manual of the Mother Church* (1895).

Mary Baker's preaching is essentially based on written literature. So in 1898, she founded Christian Science Edition and published several books such as *Christian Healing* 1886, besides popular newspapers such as *Christian Scientist Journal*, her own biography *Retrospection and Introspection* in 1891.

According to Moroccan newspaper *al-ittihad al-iShtiraki* (June 23, 2001), her movement has finally reached Morocco.

Mormons *Polygamy* **(1801-1877)**
Brigman Young who succeeded Joseph Smith led the flight of the Mormons from Illinois to Salt Lake City, Utah in defense of polygamy in 1847. This controversial issue, even among Muslims (see Dr. Aziz in *Passage to India*) is strongly embedded in the Holy Bible; in Matthew 25 you read:

Then shall the Kingdom of Heaven be likened unto ten virgins, which took their lamps, and went to meet the bridegroom. And five were wise, and five were foolish. They that were foolish took their lamps, and took no oil with them: But the wise took oil in their vessels with their lamps. While the bridegroom tarried, they all slumbered and slept. And at midnight there was a cry made, Behold, the bridegroom cometh; go ye out to meet him. Then all those virgins arose, and trimmed their lamps. And the foolish said unto the wise, give us of your oil; for our lamps are gone out. But the wise answered, saying, Not so; lest there be not enough for us and you: but go ye rather to them that sell, and buy for yourselves. And while they went to buy, the bridegroom came; and they that were ready went in with him to marriage: and the door was shut. Afterward came also the other virgins, saying, Lord, Lord, open to us. But he answered and said, Verily I say unto you, I know you not.' (King James Version)

In spite of American Constitution's ban on polygamy, the Mormon community practices(ed?) it. Their late leader Rulon T. Jeff left 20 widows, 60 children and 100 grand-children. The Mormons found strong arguments in favor of that practice in the Bible; both Old Testament (Isaiah 4:1) and New Testament (Matthew 25).

Their story started with prophet Joseph Smith in 1830 in New York. In his youth, he found some golden plates of a new Bible written in Hieroglyphics, that he succeeded in transLating into English.

The Mormons follow a gigantic search on genealogies. In their early history, they were persecuted by the Federal government that they had to take arms against. They allied some Indian tribes and moved westward until they finally settled in Salt Lake City, Utah under the leadership of Brigham Young in 1847. One of their major characteristics is that, although Christians, they do not believe in corner stone Christian principle "Original Sin!"

Jehovah's Witnesses *Jehovah* (1852-1916)
Taze Russell together with Judge Rutherford are considered as the founders of the Jehovah's Witnesses movement. This group believes in the Literal interpretation of the Bible and in implementing it in daily life. For them, Christ is only a Messenger of God!!! They are the most active fundamentalist group. They number some 4 million. Their main concern is 'The True Name of God' i.e. 'Jehovah (the Judeo-Christian name of God).

This sect (its actual name) was started by Taze Russell in 1870. it is another Church of American origin. Its followers believe that the Armageddon i.e. Second Coming of Christ, final battle between good and evil and the end of the world is near (especially the end of the present world system which they consider as satanic). It will be followed by The Millennium (a thousand years) of peace.

Its founder, Judge Rutherford, was a voracious book worm' (i.e. reader) and a prolific writer. He once stumbled on a name in the Bible and made a creed and a dynamic sect out of it. The Biblical name he came across was 'Jehovah' which tickled him so strongly that he made a religion out of it; the "only true religion" according to them.

They started in New York but have succeeded in making followers so far as Japan; including of course Europe. They had such a strong community in Nazi Germany that Hitler had to persecute them as he persecuted the Jews. They have also a strong community in Africa; especially in Nigeria. They have their own Bible that the rest of the Christians reject. They themselves reject blood transfusion, war and trinity. Each JEHOVAH witness must spend five hours a week doing door to door preaching. Their publishing activities are amazing. They have reached 10.000.000 publications in 80 languages!

Amish *'veiled women'*
This is another American Christian community/sect (?). They are traditionally a German speaking community which is

stretching from Canada in the north to US Midwestern states such as Pennsylvania and Wisconsin. They are also referred to as Mennonites after Jacob Amman (17th c).

This puritan sect rejects infant baptism, church organization, military service, public offices, oaths and modern technology. They are still driving horse carts rather than cars! Their men are moustache shaven and heavily bearded. Their women are veiled; they cook, sew and stay at home most of the time. The community lives on manual farming and herd tending.

Other Sects

Among the numberless protestant sects and groups, there are the Baptists, the Methodists, the Presbyterians, the Seventh Day Adventists, Branch Davidians, etc. Timothy MacVeigh belonged to the latter group. He was upset that the original freedom advocated by the Founding Pilgrim Fathers was suppressed by later US governments. As retaliation, he blasted the Federal Office Building in Oklahoma. Hours later, it was blamed on the Arabs!

Pentecostals generally teach that healing of the body was included in the atonement. They often have healing services and healing lines at which time they may apply oil along with prayers for healing. I have personally been in meetings where they demanded God to heal the affliction in the "name of Jesus." But in some 20 years of ministry, coming in contrast with many Pentecostal pastors and their parishioners, I have not seen any less frequency of sickness among their group.

Baptists

A major branch of evangelical Protestantism distinguished by baptizing only professing Christian believers and doing so by complete immersion. "Baptists (and I was a Baptist pastor for almost 20 years) are often extremely fatalistic when it comes to sickness. They pray very seriously and they accept treatment as a means that God uses to heal Christians who are sick. If prayers and the efforts of the medical profession don't bring healing, then that sickness is accepted as the "will of GOD." But in over 30 years of association with Baptists, I have not seen them, as a group, to have any better health than non-Baptists." (George Malkmus, *Why Christians Get Sick*)

Seventh-day Adventists (whose group was founded by Ellen G. White) have included in the teachings of their religion some very strict teachings on diet and care of the body. For instance, they teach against the use of coffee, tea, tobacco, and alcoholic beverages. One of the more interesting teachings is that they are to eat no pork and that it is best to eat no meat at all. Though the followers of this religion have not all followed these dietary teachings, statistics show that Adventists have less incidence of cancer and, in general, are healthier than the average American. Further, as a group they live six years longer than the average American.

Church of Scientology
The Church of Scientology is one of the strongest 20th c. protestant movements that are ideologically based on the dichotomy: "Messianic Preachings (+) Modern Science and technology". This Church has opted for the mixing of "religion and modem psychology." Its founder Ron Hubbard (1911-1986) advocated his method of healing, i.e. getting rid of ones past addictions and previous negative experiences, by discussion and the use of electrical devices. The goal of this is to attain a clear mind and body. Hubbard further advocated the previous "divinity of the humans" before coming to this world, which is a sort of "material prison" so to speak (cf. Plato). It is a most controversial Church, or

sect for its opponents, or even a mere commercial organization practicing the "brain washing" on its followers. Its head-quarters are based in Los Angeles (USA).
[Interestingly enough, famous actor Tom Cruise embraced its teachings in 1986, and soon after his film The Last Samurai, became a staunch preacher and defender of its beliefs. He tried to convert several VIPs of the Hollywood film industry including Steven Spielberg, and went into a hot debate with his interviewer calling him out for not understanding Scientology. This eroded much of his international fame.]

Conclusion

Is Islam the anti-thesis of Judaism and Christianism, or their complement? This article will try to give an answer.

'Say, I am no prodigy among the apostles' [The Quran 46:9]

Among the differences between Islam and Christianism are the Name of God, His Attributes, the true Prophets, how to pray, the status of women and the diet. It is usually believed that the two religions are poles apart. This study will try and bridge the gap.

1. ALLAH

His Name, Oneness and Universality
In American best-seller *Unveiling Islam*, the Caner Brothers (2002) state,
'A few days after the World Trade Center and Pentagon attacks, a memorial service was held in a baseball stadium. Thousands gathered to mourn and pray. On a large platform at the center of the infield, leaders of the gathering huddled around the

microphone. At the center stood Oprah Winfrey...She was becoming the teacher of America. All of her instruction centred in the doctrine that Islam is a peaceful and loving religion....that day in the stadium a Christian minister stood at the microphone and began the invocation, 'we pray in the name of our God –the God of Christianity, Judaism and Islam..'.

Obviously the Caners disagreed. They wondered,

'Were all the people gathered in that stadium –Christians, Jews, Muslim, and others-in fact speaking to the same 'God,' who just happens to have different nicknames...? (p.102).As far as God's Name is concerned; they argue (p.108-117) 'if a Mormon discusses the nature of God, is he or she philosophizing about Jesus Christ, Immanuel, because he or she invokes the word God? It is incumbent on us to be precise. One cannot discuss the 'name' of God without first being explicit about the nature of the God attached to the name...it is ridiculous to identify Allah with **Yahweh**...Yahweh is a caring, loving, and intimately involved father.' As a conclusion, the Caner brothers 'faced one other option; Jesus was who he said He was; **Immanuel**.'

In *The Mystery of Esther*, Frank Olsen has got many theological beliefs to propose about the 'Name of God', 'His Love', 'Jesus', 'salvation through crucifixion', 'Modernism', the 'Chosen and the Doomed People', and 'Islam and Prophet Muhammad'.

He describes God by the following attributes:

'God is Almighty, All Powerful, All-Knowing and above All Loving to his creatures and close to them.' So far so good, we agree with Frank Olsen and the Christian theology, God is further described as 'Eternal, All Knowing God (who can) conceive' (p. 113). He stresses that 'God is near you 'just seek and ye shall find.' (p. 106), that He is Merciful to 'All families' (p.118), and that 'Perfect love casts out fear' (p. 92)

He significantly stresses that 'His Holy Name is overwhelmingly important' (p.107), that

'He has torn and He will heal us (p.90). He continues in his divine descriptions, 'He has special characteristics that differentiate Him from all other beings. The expression 'God is love' keeps recurring, then Olsen leans towards a more vindictive God more akin to the God of Israel, ready to destroy their enemies like consuming fire. 'God as consuming fire' the basic differences between Biblical God and man is their characters, natures and wills.(see Jesus and God's wills at final outcry). There is a definite collision (p.53).

Olsen rightly noted that 'Jesus constantly made reference to his Father in Heaven' (p.38.) but soon contradicts himself concerning the true name of God,

'The result of Israel's final fiery furnace is the destruction of two-thirds of the nation, but the purification of one-third who call on the Name above all names. What is the name they will use that will make God respond and say, "I will hear them?" The name is "**Jesus**."' (p.129)

It is to be noted that Jesus was never accepted by the Jews not even as a Prophet, let alone as God. Besides, the name "Jesus" is the Latinized form of Esau –Jesus Himself would not recognise it, if he heard it!

So, is the Name of God: **Jesus, Yahweh, Immanuel or what?** Total confusion!

For us to defend the Islamic attributes of God including His true name i.e. *Allah* may lead others to accuse us of arrogance, bias and chauvinism. In fact the use of some words rather than others, as **Mrs. Ellen G. White** from the Seventh Day Adventist denomination noted, is crucial. It may turn that which is plain into gibberish and nonsense, 'learned men had in some instances changed the words, thinking that they were making it plain, when in reality they were mystifying that which was plain, by causing it to lean to their established views, which were covered by tradition.' (Deedat, p. 23)

There are indeed some 155 names for God if not more according to different languages and cultures (around 555 according to Caner & Caner); some of which are Khuda (India and China), Mazda, Rama, Theos, Zeus, Dios, Dia, Gud (Sweden), God (pronounced /Xod/ in Dutch), Jesus, Jehovah, Emmanuel, Eli, Eloi, Adonai, Master Mind, Master Architect (for atheists), etc., etc. What is the true Name; to be venerated?

We may find clues anywhere/everywhere!

Geographically speaking, there is an amazing world parenthesis, as it were, from 'Aloha' island in the Pacific ocean to 'Allegany' (God is rich) the sacred mountain of Native Americans (so called Red Indians).

Linguistically speaking, there are hints to the same effect. In Spanish 'Ola!' is used for welcome, 'Olle!' is an outcry of joy and satisfaction, to say 'God Willing' is expressed by 'Ojala'. In French, verb 'to go' in the first plural form is 'Allons!' which expresses future (some form of hope!) In English greetings are 'Hello' and 'Hallo!', extreme joy and satisfaction are expressed by 'Alleluya!' In Finnish, the name of God is 'Jumala' (lit. Arabic 'Day of God'))

Biblically, we find that the very first verse is quite revealing to what the name of God should be. God reveals his name in Hebrew as 'Eloh-im', (suffix –im being merely a majesty plural marker) (**Genesis 1/1**). He is a Universal God; as promised to Abraham 'you will be a blessing to all nations' (**Genesis 12/3**).

Jesus explicitly and repeatedly drew a demarcation line between him and God. He stressed the importance of sanctifying the Name of God 'Heavenly Father, let Your Name be sanctified.' (**Luke11/1**), and that 'the most important commandment is you have only ONE LORD and GOD' (**Mark 12/29-34**).

The demarcation line between Jesus and God is made crystal clear by Jesus when he said, 'the Father is greater than I am' (**John 14/28**), when he taught them how to pray, 'let Your Name be sanctified.' (**Luke11/1**) and when he cried for rescue at the end of his earthly life, 'Eli, Eli, lema sabachtani?' (**Matthew 27/46**)

In *The New Scofiled Reference Bible*, the name of God is 'Alah'.(Deedat, p.255) If this is the Scripture, the Jews, the Christians and the Muslim should think of worshipping together!

2. JESUS

Defending the 'Deity of Christ', Robert Odom (1997) states,
'The Prophet Isaiah, in the eighth century B.C., foretold the birth of the Christ, saying: "Behold a virgin shall conceive, and bear a son, and shall call his name Immanuel." Isaiah 7:14. That child's name in Hebrew means "With us God." Hence the English text of Matthew 1:23 reads: "Behold, the virgin shall be with child, and shall bring forth a son, and they shall call his name **Immanuel**, which being interpreted is, God with us." In another prophecy Isaiah wrote: "For unto us a child is born, unto us a son is given; and the government shall be upon his shoulder: and his name be called Wonderful, counsellor, Mighty God, Everlasting Father, Prince of Peace." **Isaiah 9:6**.'

This quotation is at best, self-contradictory. It can be refuted from several aspects.
First, the Jews never believed in a triune God (Caner & Caner.108) vs. God of Israel, 'you shall have no other God before Me' (Exodus 20). Second, Hebrew doesn't have capital letters (the reference could be to a mortal lord). It can further refer to Muhammad and his best friend Abu Bakr. Third, it is most likely a problem of style (the

Quran 48/9); to be interpreted metaphorically or by solving its syntactic ambiguity; viz. a problem of coordination rather than subordination is involved; this is a reference to at least two entities, i.e. a fatherless baby and God. Third, the government was never achieved by Jesus who was persecuted all his life and on the run with his disciples! Forth, some of these attributes can fit Muhammad better (See below). The mission of Jesus was uncompleted as can be seen in these self-assessments: 'I have many things to say to you, but you can't bear them now. But when he, the Spirit of Truth, comes he will guide you to all truth' (John 16/12) and 'I will send you the one promised by the Father' (Luke 24/49).

  To refute the "divinity of Christ", there are indeed some very eloquent quotations in the gospel of Matthew alone!

  When Jesus prayed to God, he called Him by His true/original Name. As we must agree that none can tell the name of God better than someone like Jesus. He cried for rescue: "Elai, Elai, lama sabachtani" (**Matthew 27/46**). This verse is agreed upon and kept by all gospels in all versions of the Bible. Amazing!

  It is also interesting to note that when it comes to the controversial expression 'son of man/son of God', Jesus himself chose 'Son of man', the most eloquent of which is,

'A teacher of the law came to him and said, "Teacher, I will follow you whenever you go." Jesus replied, "Foxes have dens and birds of the air have nests, but the Son of man has nowhere to lay his head."' (Matthew 8.20)

Concerning the controversy expression 'son of God', It is worth noting that there are a few remarks to be made. First, the expression 'son of man' far outnumbers the expression 'Son of God' (cf. St Paul). Second, the first person to call Jesus 'Son of God' was Satan (**Matthew 4:3**). Third, the second instance in which Jesus was called 'Son of God' was due to the Jews who used it in front of the Roman governor Pilate (**Matthew 26/63, 27/13**) so as to endanger Jesus' life. Forth, Jesus himself defended himself against such allegations by protesting: "that is what *you* say" (**Matthew 26/64**) (some gospels add the adverb '**rightly**' rendering it 'you rightly said it!') Fifth, at best this expression has to be read metaphorically, i.e. any person with pure heart and who makes peace will be called 'son of God' as attested in **Matthew (5:9)**: "God blesses those people who make peace. They will be called his children!" Sixth, in **Matthew 9:4** Jesus protested against those who said he was God: "why are you thinking such evil thought". Seventh, Jesus does not know the Hour –Final Judgement 'no one knows that day or hour, not even the Son or the angels in heaven' (**Matthew 24/36**). Eighth, he went to a fig tree out of season, found no fruit to eat and cursed it (**Matthew 21/19**). Ninth, when he felt his imminent death, he cried to God –the True Savior- by His Name 'Eli' (cf. above & Rev. Dr. David Jenkins & St Paul).

3. MUHAMMAD

Unknown Christian author states,

Many Muslim claim that Mohammed was foretold in earlier Scripture, i.e. the Bible, and thus Christians and Jews ought to recognise that he was the Prophet of God. To substantiate this claim, they point to several passages in the Old and New Testaments which supposedly speak of Mohammed…upon examination, however, it is quite clear that Mohammed is not discussed in these passages, and indeed, the Bible is silent about him… Genesis 49:10 "**The sceptre shall not depart** from Judah, nor a lawgiver from between his feet, until Shiloh come; and unto him shall the gathering of the people be." Muslim claim that because "Judah" is a Hebrew name which has its root in the verb "**to praise**", and because "Mohammed" means "he is to be praised" in Arabic, that this is a prophecy pointing to Mohammed. This interpretation has several fundamental flaws. First, we should note again that the name "Mohammed" does not really mean "praised one" "but chosen one"... Those Muslim who make the argument for this verse, however, miss the fact that it is not Judah who is the object of this prophecy, but the one called "Shiloh". As such, the matter of what the names "Judah" and "Mohammed" mean in their respective idioms is irrelevant. Shiloh is not so much a name as it is a title or a term of description, one which means "tranquil"...He who even in the midst of raging storm could simply say, "**Peace**"...Jesus was of the tribe of Judah, and it is indeed to Him that the **gathering of the people** was (Matthew 4:25, Luke 5:17, John 6:2), and will be in the future (Revelation 21:24). Mohammed of course, was Arab, and not Jewish, and could not have been of the tribe of Judah. Deuteronomy 18:15-18 "The LORD thy God will raise up unto thee a Prophet from the midst of thee, of thy brethren, like unto me, unto him shall ye hearken...I will raise them up a Prophet from among their brethren, like unto thee, and I will put my words in his mouth; and he shall speak unto them all that I shall command him." Muslim claim that this passage refers to Mohammed, and support this by pointing to certain copies of Septuagint (Greek Old Testament) which lacks the phrase "**from the midst of thee**"...there is no conclusive evidence that Arabs, or at least most of them, are even descended from Ishmael. We must keep in mind that the word "Arab" is not so much a specific ethnic group, but rather a description. It comes from a common **Semitic** root *crb* which has several meanings; most prominent among them are the ideas of **sterility**...in Jeremiah chapter 25, right in the middle of a list of various nations which were to be **judged by God**...In addition, archaeological evidence suggests that the descendents of Cush, a son of Ham, travelled across the Arabian peninsula during their migration from **Mesopotamia** to the region of Ethiopia...many, if not most of them, would trace their ancestry back in large part to the Hamitic line, while Ishmael was a Semite. But, I digress. This prophecy clearly points to Jesus Christ. Faithful men in Israel recognized **Jesus** as the fulfilment of this prophecy. Note their testimony, "Then those men, when they had come into the world...many of the people therefore, when they heard this saying, said, of a truth this is the Prophet." (John 6:14, 7:40). Further Jesus' actions and words demonstrated His fulfilment of this prophecy and office of that prophecy. Just as the Prophet was to have the words of God put into his mouth, so Jesus had this. "As my Father hath taught me, I speak these things" (John 8:18) – "For I have not spoken of myself; but the Father which sent me, He gave me a commandment, what I should say, and what I should speak." (John 12:49). Christ, from the tribe of Judah, was a Jew, raised up from the midst of His brethren. Hence, Jesus Christ was the complete fulfilment of Moses' prophecy in Deuteronomy.

To answer the unknown Christian author, let me start from the end. We agree with him totally concerning the last point, viz. Muslim can only give a warm applause to the conclusion he reached from the Gospels concerning the Prophethood of Jesus.
Second, if Mesopotamia means anything concerning who is Semite and who is not, it refers to the original land of the first Semite, i.e. Prophet Abraham the father of the Jews and the Arabs. Likewise the word 'Semite' is defined in any English Dictionary one chooses as , 'a member of the group of peoples who speak a Semitic language, including the Jews and Arabs'.
Third, we notice a certain animosity towards the Arabs as they are presented by the author "in Jeremiah chapter 25, right in

the middle of a list of various nations which were to be **judged by God**..."

Forth, the author shows much daring ignorance concerning the Arabic language when he states that '**Semitic** root *crb* which has several meanings; most prominent among them are the ideas of **sterility**". In authoritative Arabic Dictionary *Lisan LcArab*, Vol.1, p.592, we find exactly the opposite of his definition/claim. "Arab" simply refers to a group of people speaking the Arabic language especially the most eloquent among them. It can also, and this is important, mean a "well with abundant water!"

Fifth, the author tries to shed doubts on the Septuagint (Greek Old Testament) which lacks the phrase "**from the midst of thee**". In the Hebrew Bible, we find indeed the reference to "A Prophet from your midst" and "a Prophet from them from among their brethren". Mohammed is both "a Prophet from them" as a Semite, i.e. descendant of Abraham and "from among their brethren" as an Arab.

Sixth, If " Shiloh" is the description of one who is "tranquil» and advocates "**Peace**", . it can only apply to the Prophet of Peace, i.e. Islam.

Seventh, As far as "gathering **of the people**" (Matthew 4:25, Luke 5:17,)is concerned, Jesus had never been able to gather the Jews, let alone the people. Muhammad, by contrast, could gather 10.000 for the Victorious Conquest of Mecca alone!

Eighth, if "Judah" means 'Praise" in Hebrew as the author claims, anyone who knows Arabic knows that "Muhammad" means "**praiseworthy**" and he was indeed.

Ninth, how can the Bible be **silent** about Muhammad, when he is the most influential man that has lived on earth, and the Bible is supposed to talk about all things?

Tenth, Genesis 49:10 states, "**The sceptre shall not depart** from Judah, nor a lawgiver from between his feet, until Shiloh come; and unto him shall the gathering of the people be." It is not a definite assertion since it is negated by time adverb "until Shiloh come" and "Shiloh" as we established above means Islam

Eleventh, if the author (or any Christian or Jew for that matter) dared finishing the verse in Deuteronomy 18:15-18 he would be shivering with fear, and discover certain truths about Islam and Christianism:

"The LORD thy God will raise up unto thee a Prophet from the midst of thee, of thy brethren, like unto me; unto him shall ye hearken...I will raise them up a Prophet from among their brethren, like unto thee, and I will put my words in his mouth; and he shall speak unto them all that I shall command him. And it shall come to pass, that whosoever will not hearken unto my words which he shall speak in my name, *I will require it of him.*"

God himself will require it of him! Tremendous!

The verse continues

"But the Prophet, which shall presume to speak a word in my name, which I have not commanded him to speak, or that shall speak in the name of other Gods, even that Prophet shall die."

It substantiates a clear refutation of either the prophecy of Jesus or the Christian dogmas as Jesus was (according to Christian theology) crucified to save mankind. This verse states that only a false Prophet will be killed. By contrast there were many attempts to kill Prophet Muhammad, by throwing a heavy rock on him, by poisoning him and by drawing the swords and arrows' against him (Isaiah 21/13ff). All attempts failed. So he is and only he is the Prophet in Deuteronomy 18/18.

The name of Arabia is explicitly (?) mentioned as well as the migration of the Prophet from Mecca to Medina, 'this is the message for Arabs who live in the barren desert in the region of Dedan: you must order your caravans to bring water for those who are thirsty. You people of Tema must bring food for the hungry refugees. They are worn out and weary from being chased by enemies with the swords and arrows' (Isaiah 21/13ff)

There is also a reference to Muhammad's illiteracy.
'Now this message is like a sealed letter to you. Some of you say, 'we can't read it, because it is sealed. Others say, 'we can't read it, because we don't know how to read it.' (Isaiah 29/12)
There is a strong warning to the Jews that they would loose God's covenant as they had failed to follow the commandments. Another nation is promised (Dr. Jamal Badawi). 'I tell you that God's kingdom will be taken from you and given to people who will do what He commands' (Matthew 21/43)
Jesus made some wise prophecies and gave some warnings. These remain, however, totally ignored by most of his followers who, in his own terms, 'cannot see nor hear or understand' (Matthew 13/15). One of those warnings is found in the Story of the Ten Virgins –a warning that you should not come to truth when it is too late! (Matthew 25)
In Matthew 21/43, Jesus promised that the Kingdom of God will be

taken away from the Israelis and given to another nation. Addressing them, Jesus said, 'therefore say I unto you, the Kingdom of God shall be taken from you, and given to a nation bringing forth the fruits thereof.' Jesus promised that the Kingdom of Heaven should be given to the other branch in Abraham's family tree, i.e. the Arabs. This is in order to fulfil the promise made in Genesis 21/13

In the gospel of John 14/15-16, Jesus made his promise clearer. He said, 'if you love me keep my commandments. And I will pray the Father, and He shall give you another Paraclete' referring to another Prophet yet to come (cf. Jesus' friend). Most modern Christians consider this as a reference to the Holy Ghost, while some early Christian groups understood it as referring to a Prophet.

Besides, the scholars of the Israelites were awaiting three Prophets Jesus, Elijah and the Prophet Muhammad.

'Now this is the testimony of John when the Jews sent forth rabbis and Levites from Jerusalem to ask him, who are you? And he confessed and denied not, I am not the Christ. And they asked him, are you Elijah, he said, 'no, I am not! Are you the Prophet? He said No!" (John 1/21)

Unlike what the Christians believe, Jesus himself shows that he is not the end of the story! On several occasions, he promised another Prophet coming after him!

'I will send you the one my father has promised' (Luke 24/46)

In the last supper Jesus is foretelling the advent of the 'Paraclete' (Bucaille, 1976, p.138).

'But I tell you that I am going to do what is best for you. That is why I am going away. The Paraclete cannot come to help you until I leave. But after I am gone, I will send the spirit to you. The spirit will come and show the people of this world the truth about sin.' (John 16/7)

4. PRAYER

Caner & Caner (2002) among others have accused the Muslim of performing saturated rituals. As an answer, we may first compare that with complicated ISRAELI RITUALS: 'But he sent up in smoke the fat, the kidneys, and the lower parts of the liver from the sin offering, just as the LORD commanded Moses; the flesh and the hide he burned up outside the camp. Then he slaughtered the burnt offering. His sons handed him the blood, and he sprinkled it against the altar on all sides, etc., etc., etc.' (Levi 9:10-36). Second, Biblical; Prophets used to pray like the Muslim; bowing and going to the ground with their faces; starting with Patriarch Abraham, 'Abraham fell facedown' to thank God for the promise of a son. Moses did the same, 'Moses at once hurried to bow low to the earth and prostrate himself, then he prayed, 'lord, if really you are pleased with me, then let the lord go with us' so as to help the Israelis in the battle against the Canaanites, Hittites, etc.(Exodus 34/9). Deedat's Jewish friends once said to him, 'you're more Jewish than the Jews in your prayers!'

Actually, there is an amazing prayer in the Bible, 'I (Jehovah) will bless anyone who blesses you (Abraham)' (Genesis 12:3). In Islam, it is known as the *Abrahami Salat* (Abraham's Prayer). It is repeated, at least, five times a day by every Muslim!

Jesus, himself, taught his disciples a beautiful prayer, which is not far from *al-Fatiha*: 'Heavenly Father, let Your Name be sanctified. Give us our daily bread. And forgive our sins as we forgive others and save us from evil' (Luke11:1ff). Notice there is no trinity or salvation through blood!

5. POLYGAMY

Are women to be obedient to their husbands (as in Islam & Japanese Culture), be totally free (equal to men as in the West), or follow a compromise between the two? Is there equality in marriage (strict one-to-one relation) or Islamic polygamy?

In fact, Polygamy is a recurrent theme in the Old Testament, too. In spite of his many wives, David took a very beautiful (too) young girl at the end of his life, 'when King David was old man and well advanced in years, he could not keep warm even when they put covers over him. So his servants said to him, 'let us look for a young virgin to attend the king and take care of him. She can lie beside him so that our lord the king may keep warm.' They searched throughout Israel for a beautiful girl and found Abeshag, a Shunamite, and brought her to the king. The girl was very beautiful; she took care of the king and waited on him, but the king had no intimate relations with her.' (1Kings 1:1). The difference of age may have been some 90 (?) years. King David was so senile that he did not know her! In Isaiah, there is a reference of 7 wives to one single man!

Polygamy is again acceptable according to the New Testament, 'the kingdom of heaven is like what happened one night when *ten* girls who went to meet the bridegroom...five of them were wise and five were foolish' (Matthew 25). Fortunately, he took five only!

Ireland in the early 20th c. was polygamous. Germany?

6. VEIL

There should be some 'traffic rules' and regulations between man and woman. The Bible suggests the following hierarchy: God-Jesus-man-woman. You read in 1Corinthians 11:3-10 'now I want you to know that Christ is the head over all men, and a man is the head over the woman. But God is head over Christ'. Beautiful!

The Christian women are further required to hide their hair before going to Church, practised at least in some countries such as Ukraine, Russia, Sweden, since St Paul said, 'Hide your shame'; meaning that women should behave decently, otherwise they are exposed to continual sexual harassment (see also *Sexual Harassment in France*, L' Express 13 may, 1999)

7. DIET

Wine is believed by the Christians to be part of communion, since Jesus said, 'eat bread it's my flesh and drink wine, it's my blood' (Matthew 26: 26??)

In France, they have the tri-color flag 'bleu–blanc-rouge' referring to "liberty-equality-fraternity." Some have suggested '*gros rouge*' meaning plenty of wine on week-ends and many accidents and deadly injuries on the French roads.

St Paul is also believed to have allowed them to eat all without exception. In fact, as far as diet is concerned, Islam and the Bible seem again to agree. Concerning wine, it is said, 'do not look at wine when it exhibits its red color... at its end it bites just like a serpent' (Proverbs 23:31). Prophet Daniel refused to eat King's food or drink wine! 'But Daniel resolved not to defile himself with the royal food and wine' (Daniel 1:8)

Concerning pork eating, the Bible narrates the story of a demon-possessed man. Jesus saved him by taking out the demons from him and casting them into pigs, 'the demons began to entreat him, saying, "if you expel us, send us forth into the swine"' (Matthew 8:30)

So, eating pig is like eating demons...most revulting!

8. SWORD

Concerning the Islamic use of the sword, see Dr. Maurice Bucaille's (cf. Vatican 1970) eloquent comparison between 'Biblical *Hirim*' with 'Islamic Jihad.' The latter abides by the golden rule, 'fight for the sake of God those that fight against you, but do not attack them first' (The Quran 2:190)

9. FASTING

Fasting is to be found in both Old and New Testaments. Concerning Prophet David, you read, "David pleaded with God for the child. He fasted and went into his house and spent the nights lying on the ground" (2 Samuel 12:16).

Concerning Jesus' teaching about fasting, you read, "when you fast, do not look sombre as the hypocrites do, for they disfigure their faces to show men they are fasting. I tell you the truth, they have received their reward in full. But when you fast, put oil on your head and wash your face, so that it will not be obvious to men that you are fasting, but only your Father, who is unseen; and your Father, who sees what is done in secret, will reward you." (Matthew 6:16).

Concerning Prophets such as Barnabas, you read, 'while they were worshipping the Lord and fasting, the Holy

Spirit said, Set apart for me Barnabas and Saul for the work to which I have called them' (Acts 13:3).

Bible Succinct

'In the beginning God created the heaven and the earth.' Genesis 1:1

'And the whole earth was of one language, and of one speech' Genesis 11

'he ran to meet them from the tent door, and bowed himself toward the ground' Genesis 18:2

'Seeing that Abraham shall surely become a great and mighty nation, and all the nations of the earth shall be blessed in him?' Genesis 18:18

'And he overthrew those cities, and all the plain, and all the inhabitants of the cities, and that which grew upon the ground' Genesis 19:25

'And they made their father drink wine that night: and the first born went in, and lay with her father; and he perceived not when she lay down, nor when she arose' Genesis 19:33

'And he said, Take now thy son, thine only son Isaac, whom thou lovest, and get thee into the land of Moriah; and offer him there for a burnt offering upon one of the mountains which I will tell thee of.' Genesis 22:2

'And said unto Moses, I AM THAT I AM'('Jehovah'?) Exodus 3:14

"I will raise them up a Prophet from among their brethren, like unto thee, and I will put my words in his mouth; and he shall speak unto them all that I shall command him. And it shall come to pass, that whosoever will not hearken unto my words which he shall speak in my name, *I will require it of him.*"
Deuteronomy 18 :18

'Lo, let that night be solitary' Job 37

'And they utterly destroyed all that was in the city, both man and woman, young and old, and ox, and sheep, and ass, with the edge of the sword' Joshua 6:21

'Therefore the Lord himself shall give you a sign; behold a virgin shall conceive, and bear a son, and shall call his name Immanuel' Isaiah 7:14

'the soul that sinneth, it shall die. The son shall not bear the iniquity of the father, neither shall the father bear the iniquity of

the son: the righteousness of the righteousness shall be upon him, and the wickedness of the wicked shall be upon him.'
Ezekiel 18:20

'The burden upon Arabia' Isaiah 2113

'And I shall shake all nations, and the desire of all nations shall come' Haggai 2:7

'His mouth is most sweet: yea, he is altogether lovely. This is my beloved, and this is my friend, O daughters of Jerusalem.'
Songs of Solomon 5:16

'But when he saw many of the Pharisees and Sadducees come to his baptism, he said unto them, O generation of vipers, who hath warned you to flee from the wrath to come?' Matthew 37

'It is written, Man shall not live by bread alone, but by every word that proceedeth out of the mouth of God.'
Matthew 4:4

'Ye are the salt of the earth: but if the salt have lost his savour, wherewith shall it be salted' Matthew 5:13

'Think not that I am come to destroy the law, or the prophets: I am not come to destroy, but to fulfil' Matthew 5:17

'But I say unto you, That ye resist not evil: but whosoever shall smite thee on thy right cheek, turn the other also' Matthew 5:39

'Take therefore no thought for the morrow: for the morrow shall take thought of things of itself.' Matthew 6:34

'And why beholdest thou the mote that is in thy brother's eye, but considerest not the beam that is in thine own eye?' Matthew 7:3

'Give not that which is holy unto the dogs, neither cast ye your pearls before swine,' Matthew 7:6

<u>'Therefore all things whatsoever ye would that men should do to you, do ye even so to them: for this is the law and the prophets.' Matthew 7:12</u>

'The foxes have holes, and the birds of the air *have* nests, but the Son of man hath not where to lay *his* head.' Matthew 8:20

'So the devils besought him saying, If thou cast us out, suffer us to go away into the herd of swine.' Matthew 8:31

'Yea; have ye never read, Out of the mouth of babes and sucklings thou hast perfected praise?' Matthew 21:16

'And all things, whatsoever ye shall ask in prayer, believing, ye shall receive.' Matthew 21:22

'And when he saw a fig tree in the way, he came to it, and found nothing thereon, but leaves only, and said unto it, Let no fruit grow on the henceforward for ever.' Matthew 21:19

'Therefore say I unto you, The kingdom of God shall be taken from you, and given to a nation bringing forth the fruits thereof.' Matthew 21:43

'But of that day and hour knoweth no *man*, no, not the angels of heaven, but my Father only.' Matthew 24:36

'Verily I say unto thee, That this night, before the cock crow, thou shalt deny me thrice.' Matthew 26:34

'Put up again thy sword into his place: for all they that take the sword shall perish with the sword.' Matthew 26:52

'When Pilate saw that he could prevail nothing, but *that* rather a tumult was made, he took water, and washed *his* hands before the multitude, saying, I am innocent of the blood of this just person: see ye *to it*.' Matthew 27:24

'Go ye therefore, and teach all nations, baptizing them in the name of the Father, and of the Son, and of the Holy Ghost.' Matthew 28:19

'Eloi, Eloi, lama sabachthani? which is, being interpreted, My God, my God, why hast thou forsaken me?' Marc 15:34

'And a certain ruler asked him, saying, Good Master, what shall I do to inherit eternal life? And Jesus said unto him, Why callest thou me good? None is good, save one, that is, God.' Luke 1818

'But those mine enemies, which would not that I should reign over them, bring hither, and slay them before me.' Luke19:27

'And, behold, I send the promise of my Father upon you: but tarry ye in the city of Jerusalem, until ye be endued with power from on high.' Luke 24:49

'And this is the record of John, when the Jews sent priests and Levites from Jerusalem to ask him, Who art thou? And he confessed, and denied not; but confessed, I am not the Christ. And they asked him, What then? Art thou Elias? And he saith, I am not. Art thou that prophet? And he answered, No.' John 1:21

'Fill the waterpots with water. And they filled them up to the brim. And he saith unto them, Draw out now, and bear unto the governor of the feast. And thy bare it. When the ruler of the feast had tasted the water that was made wine.' John 2:9

'For God so loved the world, that he gave his only begotten Son, that whosoever believeth in him should not perish, but have everlasting life.' John 3:16

'If he called them gods ' John 10:35

'I am the way, the truth, and the life: no man cometh unto the Father, but by me.' John 14:6

'for my Father is greater than I.' John 14:28

'And when he is come, he will reprove the world of sin, and of righteousness, and of judgment:' John 16:8

'Peace be upon you: as my Father hath sent me, even so I send you.' John 20:21

"Saul, Saul, why persecutest thou me?" Acts 9:4

'for if the truth of God hath more abounded through my lie unto his glory; why yet am I also judged as a sinner?' Romans 3:7

'I say therefore to the unmarried and widows, it is good for them if the abide even as I.' I Corinthians 7:8

'I am alpha and omega, the first and the last.' Revelation 1:8

'And the winepress was trodden without the city, and blood came out of the winepress, even unto the horse bridles, by the space of a thousand and six hundred furlongs.' Revelation 14:20

'And he gathered them together into a place called in the Hebrew tongue Armageddon.' Revelation 16:16

History Succinct

Jesus Christ (33)
Saint Paul (62)
Nero burns Roma and blames Christians 68
Constantine the Great crushes Ariusians
Jerome translates Bible into Latin 420
Orthodox break with Catholics 1054
Pope urban II starts Crusades 1095
Saladin faces King Richard 1187
Queen Isabella established Inquisition
Martin Luther (1483-1546) translates Bible into German
Henry VIII breaks with Catholic Church
K.J.V. 1611
Napoleon invades Egypt 1799
France invades Algeria 1830
Bosnian genocide 1993
Pope Benedict XVI attacks the Prophet 2006

Glossary

Armageddon
A place in Palestine in which the final battle between good and evil will take place, between Jesus and Satan. Blood will flow like rivers. Revelation 14:20, 16:16

Attila (453)
A Han leader who destroyed Rome. the Pope fled, paying him a tax.

Augustine 430
One of the first fathers of the church in north Africa. His teachings influenced both Catholics and protestants

Bible
An encyclopedia of books varying according to Jewish and Christian traditions, considered as inspired by God. in the 3rd century BC. the Jewish doctors established the 1st Greek version of the Bible called Septuagint.
'the original copies and the most ancient copies have all perished. RSV 52 and 71 only versions to reach most ancient manuscripts, then came the vulgate, the KJV 1611, ...in the above drawing is shown the gradual development of the English Bible as well as the foundations upon which each

successive version rests. We are living in the age of printing. It is hard for us to realize that when the books of the Bible were originally written, thee was no printing press to multiply the copies. Each copy must be made slowly and laboriously by hand. Under these conditions it was inevitable that many ancient books should be lost. This largely accounts for the fact that all the original manuscripts of the Bible have perished. The question arises: what have we then as the literary foundation of our Bible? 1. we have the most ancient copies made from the original manuscripts. We mention only three principle ones: a) the Codex Sinaiticus, originally a codex of the Greek Bible belonging to the fourth century. b) The Codex Alexandrianus, probably written in the fifth century, now in the British Museum. It contains the whole Greek Bible with the exception of the four lost leaves. c) The Codex Vaticanus, in the Vatican library at Rome, originally contained the whole Bible but parts are lost. Written probably about the fourth century.' (Deedat, , p. 20)

    Bluetooth 950
    First Danish king who accepted christianism

Bugeau (1840-1847)
French army leader who invaded several algerian villages with his army and catholic priests. He turned mosques into churches. He invaded Morocco at Isly 1844

Confirmation
A rite in several Christian churches that confirms a baptized person in his faith and admits him to full participation in the church.

Confession
The act of a penitent accusing himself of his sins.

Coptic Church
From pharaonic origin. It numbers 7 million Egyptian whose ancestors converted in the 3rd c. and split with the catholic in 451, over a row about the nature of Christ

Indulgences
Remission of a temporal punishment for a sin after guilt has been forgiven.

KKK
A secret Christian fraternity in the USA. It was a violent racist organization specialised in lynching the blacks [Malcolm X]

Maronites
Followers of Maron (667) who believed that Christ had two natures. He was excommunicated in 680 in Constantinople. In 1811 the catholic church reconciled them. They faced the Druze of Lebanon

Mother Theresa (1910-1997)
Indian catholic nun who devoted her life and energy to humanitarian causes and preaching ever since the year 1937 in Calcutta

Deedat (1917-2005)
Muslim scholar specialized in comparative religion from south Africa. He met the biggest missionaries of the world in public debates. He was born in a poor Indian family although he originally belonged to a Brahma family (). They had to migrate to south Africa. He worked for a considerate Jew and was continually under the assault of the Christian missionaries of Adam's mission. They usually attacked Prophet Muhammad in front of him. he was suffering not to be able to defend, the man h loved more than himself.' Until he read Truth Revealed by another great Indian scholar called Rahmatullah.

Deedat's thought can be summarized in a three-fold criticism: criticism of christianism, criticism of the Bible and criticism of the Muslims' attitude.

His criticism of the Bible a based on a scientific approach defying by logic and linguistic principles. He faced Jimmy Swaggart, Robert Douglas, Stanley Shoebert and others in the subjects Is the Bible God's Word, Crucifixion or Cruci-fiction, etc. he suggested an open debate to Pope in Rome. the latter suggest a face to face in his own office. The debate did not take place!

Friends
From the Quakers' origin founded by George Fox 1650. They have dropped all rituals and are open to any form of worship, helping in social matters.

Graham Bill (1918-)
American pastor considered as the Pope of the Protestants. He preached to more than 20 million people each year. He was the spiritual adviser of America according to 'Who's Who?'

King James
Born June 19, 1566, Edinburgh, Scotland—died March 27, 1625, Hertfordshire, England. He was
the king of Scotland (as James VI) from 1567 and first Stuart king of England from

1603 until his death in 1625. He styled himself "king of Great Britain." James was a strong advocate of royal absolutism, and his conflicts with an increasingly self-assertive Parliament set the stage for the rebellion against his successor, Charles I. In addition, James famously oversaw a new authorized English translation of the Bible, published in 1611, which became known as **the King James Version**

Jehovah
The name of God revealed to Moses on mount Horeb

David Jenkins
David Edward Jenkins (1925-2016) a Church of England Cleric. He was Bishop of Durham 19841994. After his retirement he continued to serve as a Honorary Assistant Bishop of Leeds Diocese. He rejects the divinity of Jesus. (DAILY NEWS 25/6/84)

HIRIM
A Hebrew word meaning mass killing of men, women, children, etc. Josuha 6:21

Malkmus
An American missionary who lived the dilemma of seeing his fellow Christians 'the best Group of people' suffer and die of cancer, stroke, diabetes, etc.

Marist: a worshipper of Mary

Mary:
Hail Mary full of grace
The Lord is with thee,
Blessed art thou among women
And blessed is the fruit of
Thy womb Jesus,
Holy Mary Mother of God
Pray for us sinners
Now and at the hour of our death.
Amen!

Modernism
This movement was initiated from the Catholic church by the end of the 19th c. Its propellers tried to reconcile philosophical, historical and psychological theories with the catholic dogmas. Cardinal Frances condemned them.

Moral Majority
Conservative Christian Middle class in the US led by Bush, that stands for religion, moral values, family, etc. against abortion, homosexuality, human cell experiments, etc.

Paraclete
The defender, see John 16:14 & Maurice Bucaille

Paul : « St Paul a fait le tournant à 150% du Christianisme de la culture Judéo-araméenne à la culture grecque. » Joseph Lépine

Sunday School
American and European schools that teach Christian principles to the kinds on Sundays and tech the history of Palestine as it is taught in Israel

666 Beast
This Last Days Beast is mentioned in Revelation 17:13. some Protestants believe that it refers to the Pope

Sylvester II 999-1003
A pope who studied at Quraween in Fes

Traduttore, Traditore (translator, traitor)
Italian aphorism which means that all translations are fatally untrustworthy. They betray the idea of the author.

Victor Hugo 1802-1885
Leader of the romantic school in France, author of La Dame de Paris, Les Miserables, etc. Some claim he was a secret Muslim

Williams Rowan (08-02-2008) archbishop of Canterbury talks in favor of Islamic Law.

Bibliography

Akkad, Mustafa, *The Message* (film)

Ata ur-Rahim M. *Jesus, a Prophet of Islam*, MWH, London, 1979

Barbouch Mimoun, *Leopold Weiss' Road to Mecca*, ms Oujda, 2006

BenHamza Mouhamed, *Mohamed Messager de Dieu*, Arayhane, 1990

Ben Rochd *Islamic Thought*, ms, Oujda, 1990

Ben Rochd *Islam in the West*, ms, Oujda, 1990

Ben Rochd, *Muhammad*, Andalusia, 2006

Bucaille Maurice *La Bible, Le Coran et La Science*, Seghers, Paris, 1976

Caner & Caner *Unveiling Islam*, Kregel, Grand Rapids, MI, 2002

Dawood *The Qur'an*, Penguin, 2003

Deedat Ahmed *The Choice*, MWH, London, 1986

Garaudy Roger *PRomesses de l'Islam*, Seuil, Paris 1981

Garaudy Roger *L'Affaire Israel*, Papyrus, Paris 1983

Guillaume Alfred *Islam*, Penguin, 1977

Guillaume Alfred *The Life of Muhammad*, OUP, 1982

Halley Alex *The Autobiography of Malcolm X*, Penguin, London, 1966

Hart Michael *The 100: A Ranking of the Most Influential Persons in History*, Citadel Press, NY, 1995

Hunke Sigrid, *Allahs Sonne Uber Dem Abendland*, Stuttgart 1964

Stuttgart, 1964

Huntington Samuel, "The West : Unique, Not Universal," Harvard University, 1996

Kaidi Lotfi *L'Islam*, Hachette, Paris, 1988

Kalisky Rene *L'origine et l'essor du monde Arabe*, MArabout, Paris,1974

Kasimirski, Le Coran, Garnier-Flamarion, 1970

King James Version of the Holy Bible, 1611

Miller William, *A Christian Response to Islam*, Tyndale, IL, 1980

Mufassir, Muhammad in the Bible, MIS, 1732

Nietzsche; F. 1967 *L'Anté-Christ*, 1018, Paris

Pickthall M.M. *The Meaning of the Glorious Qur'an*, Mentor, NY

Quinn Bob, *The Atlantean Irish*, Dublin, 2005

Rodinson Maxime, *Mahomet*, Seuil, Paris, 1961

Virgil, C. G., *Vie de Mahomet*, Plon, 1962

Weiss Leopold, The *Road to Mecca*, Simon & Schuster Inc., NY, 1954

Yallop, David, A. *Deliver Us from Evil: The Yorkshire Ripper*, Futura, London, 1981

Yusuf Ali, *The Meaning of the Holy Qur'an*, USA, 1992.

Yusuf Islam, *The Life of the Last Prophet*, London.(CD)

© 2024 El Mouatamid Ben Rochd
Publish : BoD – Books on Demand, info@bod.fr
Impression : BoD – Books on Demand, In de Tarpen 42, Norderstedt (Allemagne)
Print on demand
ISBN : 978-2-3225-3705-1
Legal Deposit : April 2024